KATHY and DAVID BLACKW

SOLO TIME FOR CELLO

BOOK 2

Contents

Grateful thanks are due to Alison Ingram for all her help with this collection.

Audio: there are full performances and piano-only backings for each piece in this collection at www.oup.com/solocello2. Audio credits: Laura Anstee (cello), David Blackwell (piano), Ken Blair (producer/engineer for BMP The Sound Recording Company Ltd.). Recorded at the Holywell Music Room, Oxford.

Repeats are not observed in the recordings, except for No. 5; Da Capos and Dal Segnos are observed.

OXFORD
UNIVERSITY PRESS

Great Clarendon Street, Oxford OX2 6DP, England.
This collection and each individual work within it © Oxford University Press 2022.
Unauthorized arrangement or photocopying of this copyright material is ILLEGAL.

Kathy and David Blackwell have asserted their right under the Copyright, Designs and Patents Act, 1988, to be identified as the Authors of this Work.

ISBN 978-0-19-355067-4
Music and text origination by Julia Bovee
Printed in Great Britain

1. Aria in F

from Cantatas BWV 208 and BWV 68

Johann Sebastian Bach (1685–1750)
arr. KB & DB

Bach used the music of this aria in two cantatas: first in his so-called 'Hunt' Cantata, BWV 208, a secular work from 1713, and secondly in BWV 68, a sacred piece written 12 years later. In both there is a significant instrumental part that is the equal of the soprano solo: in BWV 208 it's for cello and in BWV 68 for 'violoncello piccolo'—an instrument difficult to pin down but smaller than a cello and probably with an extra string, enabling it to play in a higher range. Our version conflates the two: it follows the form of 208 but borrows Bach's folk-like melody from 68 (cello, bars/measures 5–8) to make a joyful duo for cello and piano.

2. A Song for August

Kathy and David Blackwell

This gentle piece is written in AABA song form, used in many popular songs. Imagine it as a 'song without words' to help shape the phrases. Aim for smooth bow changes and a rich singing tone over the range of the cello. Enjoy exploring the expressive and lyrical qualities of the cello, and be sure to leave something more to give in bars 61–3 where the melody reaches its peak.

3. Sugar with Cinnamon

Lavildevan
arr. KB & DB

Lavildevan was a Brazilian composer active at the end of the nineteenth century, and known only by his surname. Brazilian dance music of this time was a blend of European and Afro-Caribbean musical styles, with the regular phrases and clear harmonic structure of European dances enriched by the traditional rhythms of Latin-American dance music, here represented by the *cinquillo* (the five-note rhythm found e.g. in bar 23) and

the *habanera* (the characteristic rhythm from the Cuban dance of the same name, heard in bar 25 and throughout the piano accompaniment). This blend gives rise to the title of this piece, with 'sugar' and 'cinnamon' standing for white and black musical characteristics. Be careful to contrast the *cinquillo* and triplet rhythms when side by side. A number of bars start with a rest—be sure not to hold on the note from the previous bar.

4. Élégie

from Op. 18 No. 2

Teresa Carreño (1853–1917)
arr. KB & DB

The Venezuelan pianist and composer Teresa Carreño enjoyed an international career as a virtuoso pianist, giving concerts world-wide. She began composing and performing from an early age, and in 1863 performed at the White House for Abraham Lincoln, the President of the United States. Craters on the planet Venus are named after women who have made a significant contribution to their field, and so it's fitting that Teresa Carreño, a successful female composer and outstanding performer, has a crater named after her. This poignant piece, originally written for piano, is a funeral elegy with an expressive and moving melody.

5.   Song without Words

Op. 19 No. 1

Felix Mendelssohn (1809–47)
arr. KB & DB

Often considered to be one of the finest composers of the Romantic era, Mendelssohn wrote symphonies, concertos, chamber music, and numerous pieces for solo piano. His most famous works for piano are his many *Lieder ohne Worte*, 'Songs without words'—short lyrical piano pieces characterized by expressive melodic writing and rich romantic harmonies. There are no actual words to these pieces, but the melodic phrases suggest a song-like line, and imagining where a singer might breathe will help shape the lyrical and expressive phrases.

6.   Romance No. 1

Elfrida Andrée (1841–1929)
arr. KB & DB

Elfrida Andrée was a Swedish composer and conductor and also one of the first female organists to be appointed in Scandinavia, becoming the organist of Gothenburg Cathedral in 1867. She was active in the women's movement and campaigned for a change in the law to allow women to apply for the position of cathedral organists. Among her compositions are chamber and orchestral music, choral and instrumental works, and two organ symphonies. This piece, originally written for violin and piano, is typical of her romantic musical style, with a lyrical and expressive melody and rich harmony.

7. Puck

from *Lyric Pieces*, Op. 71 No. 3

Edvard Grieg (1843–1907)
arr. KB & DB

This piece is from the last volume of Grieg's *Lyric Pieces*, a collection of 66 pieces for solo piano published in ten books. It is a character sketch for the impish sprite and mischievous prankster from Shakespeare's *A Midsummer Night's Dream*, and a sense of fantasy, with a hint of menace, runs through the piece. Closely observing the articulations and dynamics will help convey the character of this piece.

8. Rondo

from Sonata for bassoon and cello, K292

Wolfgang Amadeus Mozart (1756–91)
arr. KB & DB

a piacere

This piece is abridged and adapted from the last movement of a sonata for two bass instruments. The sonata is something of a puzzle. It may have been intended as a piece for solo instrument and keyboard (with the keyboard player improvising an accompaniment from the bass line), and some scholars have questioned whether it was written by Mozart. Even so, it remains an exciting and exuberant work, filled with characteristics of the Classical style. A rondo is a piece with a main theme (here bars 1–10), which reappears several times in the home key, interspersed with contrasting episodes, usually in different keys. At the end of episodes players would improvise a short cadenza (known as an 'Eingang', from the German word for 'entrance') that led back to the main rondo theme. These are shown in small notes in bars 36 and 62.

9. Slavonic Dance

from 'American' Suite, Op. 98

Antonin Dvořák (1841–1904)

arr. KB & DB

This piece by the great Czech composer Dvořák is the fifth movement of his 'American' Suite (so-called because Dvořák was in America when he wrote it). It was originally written for piano in 1894 then orchestrated over the following year. In the Suite this movement has no title, but it has many of the features of traditional Czech folk music, which Dvořák often used in his compositions. Contrast the vitality of the opening minor section with the tenderness of the D major section. Omit the repeat of the first section on the D.𝄋.

10. Jota

No. 4 of *Siete canciones populares españolas*

Manuel de Falla (1876–1946)
arr. KB & DB

The composer Manuel de Falla is considered one of the most important Spanish composers of the early twentieth century, writing orchestral, vocal, and instrumental music and works for the stage. His music vividly captures the colour and vibrancy of Spain, and he often incorporated the rhythms, melodic phrases, and style of traditional Spanish music. This piece is from a set of seven popular Spanish songs, composed in 1914. A Jota (pronounced 'hota', with 'h' as in Scottish 'loch') is a lively traditional Aragonese dance in triple time, often sung and danced to the accompaniment of castanets and guitars, suggested here in the piano accompaniment. In de Falla's setting the singer only sings in the *poco meno vivo* sections, and the text is actually a tender love song. Contrast the more lyrical mood of these sections with the lively 3/8 rhythms that surround it.

11. Deep River

from Op. 59 No. 10

Samuel Coleridge-Taylor (1875–1912)
arr. KB & DB

Samuel Coleridge-Taylor was an English composer, conductor, and violinist who began studying at the Royal College of Music in London at the age of fifteen, where he was taught composition by Stanford. His Symphony in A minor was written while a student at the College, and its first performance there included Holst on trombone and Vaughan Williams on triangle. His later cantata *Hiawatha's Wedding Feast*, based on an epic poem by Henry Longfellow, was hugely popular and frequently performed in Britain and around the world. 'Deep River' is an arrangement of a piece originally written for piano from a collection of twenty-four pieces based on spirituals. In his introduction, the composer said his aim was to integrate traditional African music into the classical tradition in the same way as composers such as Brahms had done with Hungarian folk music.

12. Allegro

from Sonata, Op. 1 No. 6

Francesca Lebrun (1756–91)

arr. KB & DB

Francesca Lebrun was an eighteenth-century German composer and opera singer renowned for her vocal range and virtuosity. This Allegro is an arrangement of a movement from a series of six keyboard sonatas originally written for harpsichord or piano with violin accompaniment. It displays many of the features of the Classical style: fast scale and arpeggio passages, clear harmonies, and cadential trills that should begin on the upper note. She was born and died in the same years as Mozart.

13. Nulla in mundo pax sincera

from RV 630

Antonio Vivaldi (1678–1741)
arr. KB & DB

This is an arrangement of part of a sacred motet for soprano and strings by one of the most well-known composers of the Italian baroque era, Antonio Vivaldi. It uses the characteristic lilting rhythm of a siciliana, a dance form usually in a slow 6/8 or 12/8 time and popular in the seventeenth and eighteenth centuries. Thought to have originated in Sicily, it was a form widely used in Baroque arias and sonatas. The title translates as 'There is no true peace left in the world', yet, as the music suggests, peace can be attained through trust in Christ. The motet was used to great effect as part of the soundtrack to the 1996 film *Shine*, a biopic about the Australian pianist David Helfgott.

14. Adagio Cantabile

No. 2 of *Cinnamon Grove*

Robert Nathaniel Dett (1882–1943)
arr. KB & DB

The Canadian composer Robert Nathaniel Dett was one of the first black composers to integrate African-American music and spirituals into his compositions. Although born in Canada, he spent most of his professional life studying and working in America as a choral conductor, concert pianist, and teacher. This piece, the second movement from a suite for piano, is typical of Dett's romantic musical language and displays some highly original harmonic touches. It is prefaced with these words by the Bengali writer Rabindranath Tagore, the first non-European to win the Nobel prize for literature (in 1913): '*When thou commandest me to sing it seems that my heart would break with pride, and I look to thy face, and tears come to my eyes*'.

15. Adagio and Allegro
from Sonata, Op. 2 No. 6

Benedetto Marcello (1686–1739)
arr. KB & DB

Benedetto Marcello was an Italian Baroque composer of both instrumental and choral works. Born in Venice into an aristocratic family, he combined a career as a composer with a career in law in the service of the Venetian republic. His six sonatas for cello and basso continuo, first published in 1732, are attractive, tuneful, and well-written for the instrument, and have been enduringly popular with players. These are the opening two movements of the last sonata, offering a lyrical, 'singing' Adagio followed by a lively, fleet-footed Allegro. Trills should begin on the upper note. Where fingering is given with a trill, fingering is shown for both the upper note and the principal note, e.g. Adagio bar 2, '4 2' indicates a trill on D and C.

16. Elegy

Op. 8 No. 3

Laura Valborg Aulin (1860–1928)
arr. KB & DB

The Swedish composer and pianist Laura Valborg Aulin was born into a musical family, with her mother a singer and her father a keen amateur violinist. She began piano lessons with her grandmother and entered the Royal Swedish Academy of Music at the age of seventeen, studying both piano and composition. Her compositions include two string quartets, vocal works, and music for solo piano. This Elegy is from a set of seven pieces for piano, Op. 8. As with many of her shorter pieces, the title conveys the character and mood of the music. It was transcribed for violin and piano by her brother Tor, who was also a composer.

KATHY and DAVID BLACKWELL

SOLO TIME FOR CELLO
BOOK 2

Piano accompaniment book

Contents

Grateful thanks are due to Alison Ingram for all her help with this collection.

OXFORD
UNIVERSITY PRESS

Great Clarendon Street, Oxford OX2 6DP, England.
This collection and each individual work within it © Oxford University Press 2022.
Unauthorized arrangement or photocopying of this copyright material is ILLEGAL.

Kathy and David Blackwell have asserted their right under the Copyright, Designs and Patents Act,
1988, to be identified as the Authors of this Work.

ISBN 978-0-19-355067-4
Music and text origination by Julia Bovee
Printed in Great Britain

1. Aria in F

from Cantatas BWV 208 and BWV 68

Johann Sebastian Bach (1685–1750)
arr. KB & DB

4

2.   A Song for August

Kathy and David Blackwell

3. Sugar with Cinnamon

Lavildevan
arr. KB & DB

9

4. Élégie

from Op. 18 No. 2

Teresa Carreño (1853–1917)

arr. KB & DB

un poco più mosso

rit.   meno mosso   rall.   D.𝄋 al Coda

CODA

rall.

5. Song without Words

Op. 19 No. 1

Felix Mendelssohn (1809–47)
arr. KB & DB

6. Romance No. 1

Elfrida Andrée (1841–1929)
arr. KB & DB

7. Puck

from *Lyric Pieces*, Op. 71 No. 3

Edvard Grieg (1843–1907)
arr. KB & DB

19

8. Rondo

from Sonata for bassoon and cello, K292

Wolfgang Amadeus Mozart (1756–91)

arr. KB & DB

9.   Slavonic Dance

from 'American' Suite, Op. 98

Antonin Dvořák (1841–1904)
arr. KB & DB

10. Jota

No. 4 of *Siete canciones populares españolas*

Manuel de Falla (1876–1946)
arr. KB & DB

31

11. Deep River

from Op. 59 No. 10

Samuel Coleridge-Taylor (1875–1912)
arr. KB & DB

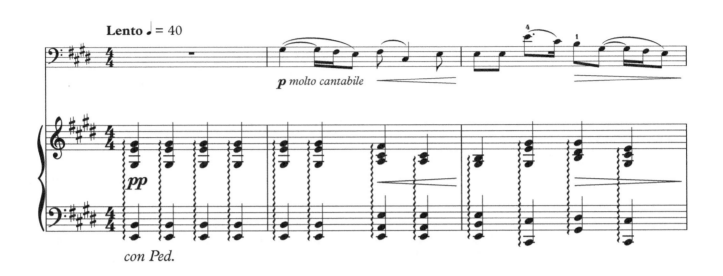

12. Allegro

from Sonata, Op. 1 No. 6

Francesca Lebrun (1756–91)
arr. KB & DB

40

42

13. Nulla in mundo pax sincera

from RV 630

Antonio Vivaldi (1678–1741)
arr. KB & DB

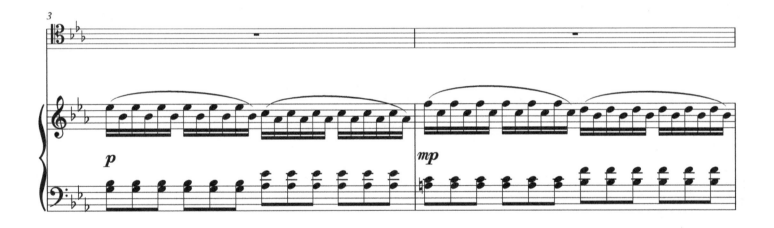

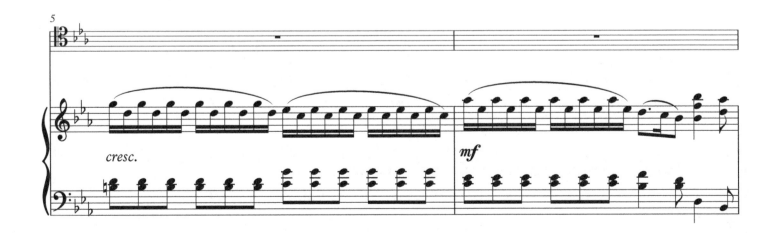

14. Adagio Cantabile

No. 2 of *Cinnamon Grove*

Robert Nathaniel Dett (1882–1943)

arr. KB & DB

50

15. Adagio and Allegro
from Sonata, Op. 2 No. 6

Benedetto Marcello (1686–1739)
arr. KB & DB

16. Elegy

Op. 8 No. 3

Laura Valborg Aulin (1860–1928)

arr. KB & DB